DAMP SQUIDS
& CARD SHARKS

**A Compendium of Commonly Confused
Phrases and Linguistic Muddles**

Robert Anwood
illustrations by Daniel Rieley

Hardie Grant
QUADRILLE

contents

introduction

Born from a blend of other languages and influenced by cultures from around the world, the English language is a reflection of the humans who created it and the billion-plus who use it today: brilliant and infuriating; venerable yet idiotic; somehow both predictable and unpredictable at the same time.

No one *really* agrees on the rules. Certain general notions of how English words 'should' be written, pronounced or used are enforced by teachers, parents, dictionaries and syllabuses (or should that be 'syllabi'?) — but those notions change from country to country, region to region, speaker to speaker, year to year.

Despite this, *you* know when someone has just said something wrong, don't you? That's because *you're right* and they're not, and they sound ridiculous and you don't. *Of course* it's 'avocado' and not 'advocado',

you explain. But get down from your high horse
– especially if your horse has been chomping
at the bit – because we all get English wrong,
all the time. There are so many mistakes out there:
malapropisms (also known as dogberryisms),
eggcorns, mondegreens, misspellings (or should
that be 'mispellings'?), misattributions, misquotes,
misprints, mispronunciations, mistranslations,
Miss Congeniality 2.

This book isn't a finger-wagging correctional guide,
but a celebration of the stuff we all get wrong. If you
learn something along the way, great – but mainly
it's designed to make you smile. I promise there's no
test at the end.

Robert Anwood

May 2023

one foul swoop

The correct form of this phrase, about accomplishing several actions all at the same time, is 'one fell swoop'. The adjective 'fell' is unusual, meaning 'fierce', 'cruel' or 'intense', which is why it is often assumed to be the more familiar 'foul'. But if you did something at (or in) one foul swoop it would be pretty disgusting, like a seagull zooming in to defecate on a hapless tourist's head.

The phrase was popularised by Shakespeare in *Macbeth*, where Macduff is informed that his wife and children have been slaughtered. (If you're unfamiliar with *Macbeth*, I can confirm that it's an upbeat, feelgood show which usually has the audience dancing in the aisles on their way out.) Macduff invokes the avian imagery of a 'hell-kite' which has murdered his 'pretty chickens and their damme at one fell swoop'.

Another phrase with a similar meaning is 'to kill two birds with one stone', originating from the use of slingshots in hunting. I don't know what it is about killing birds and getting things done, but I'm glad I've been able to enlighten you about both idioms in one fowl swoop.

blessing in the skies

I reckon most people think that if God is anywhere, he's somewhere up in the skies, so it makes perfect sense that if something turns out to be a blessing, that's where it could happen. (I use the pronoun 'he' based on conventional usage. However, as I have never received an email from God and haven't been able to find God's LinkedIn profile – presumably God has set it to private and is not open to work right now – I can't say with certainty how God self-identifies.)

The point about this idiom, however, is not where a blessing takes place, but the fact that it *is* a blessing, because the actual saying is 'blessing in disguise', used to describe something which seemed awful but turns out to be great.

The origin of this phrase is credited to James Hervey, in his hymn 'Since All the Downward Tracts of Time'. Hervey isn't on LinkedIn, either – he lived in the eighteenth century – but I feel sure his occupation would have been *Bestselling Author | Visionary Hymn-Wrangler | C-Level Thought Leader | Seasoned Anglican Priest | Memoir Ninja | Graveyard School Poet | Change Manager.*

PIN number

'I've forgotten my PIN number,' you sigh, standing in front of the ATM. So you look it up on your phone, even though you know you weren't supposed to write it down anywhere, physically or electronically, because someone is probably looking over your shoulder right now.

Suddenly you realise the person looking over your shoulder isn't a thief but a pedant, shouting that you don't need to say 'PIN number', because the acronym 'PIN' stands for 'personal identification number' – so it's like saying 'personal identification number number'.

'Go away and let me use the ATM machine in peace,' you reply.

The pedant then explains that you don't need to say 'ATM machine' because the acronym 'ATM' stands for 'automatic teller machine' – so it's like saying 'automatic teller machine machine'.

You wrestle the pedant to the ground in an argument about whether 'ATM' is an acronym, an initialism or simply an abbreviation, while the machine ejects your card because you didn't enter your PIN number in time.

shoe-in

Have you ever found yourself trying to scare birds or other animals away by frantically waving your arms towards them? If so, you were shooing them away – and you might even have shouted 'Shoo!' as you did so. If you thought you were shouting 'Shoe!' then you were wrong, unless you were taking things to the next level by hurling your footwear at them.

It's from the idea of shooing animals into something that we get 'shoo-in', meaning someone or something certain to succeed. In horse-racing a 'shoo-in' originally meant the winner of a rigged race; the term later lost its connotations of rigging and simply came to mean any horse certain to win – although, clearly, if any concept of certainty actually existed in horse-racing, no one would bet on it.

Eventually 'shoo-in' took on a more general sense to describe a candidate (especially in political or business life) who should be certain to win, and from there, anything which should be a certainty.

peak my interest

It sounds logical, doesn't it, that if something has attracted your attention, then your interest has 'peaked'?

However, the correct phrase doesn't refer to the level of your interest but to the fact that your interest has been stimulated in the first place. Although pronounced in the same way, when you see the correct spelling written down, you can hazard a guess that 'pique' comes from the French – where *piquer* means 'sting' – so in English, your interest is piqued by something catching your attention.

While we're at it, you also can't write that something has 'peeked' your interest. That would refer to something taking a sneaky look at your interest, which makes no sense at all, given that your interest isn't something visible.

Overall, if you're struggling with any of this, I have some very simple advice, which I sometimes wish I'd followed myself: *never right anything down*.

statue of limitations

Armchair lawyers love to confidently cite this to demonstrate their expert knowledge of the legal system. It doesn't matter *which* legal system: you simply can't get done for a crime that happened more than twelve years ago, because it's beyond the statue of limitations – everyone knows that.

First and foremost, it's 'statute', not 'statue'. The extra 't' changes it from a sculpture to a legal document. And the fact that it's a legal document means that it can't be a general concept across the whole world: a statute is enacted in a specific country or state to put the rules for that jurisdiction in place.

Consequently, a statute of limitations does define the maximum time limit for pursuing legal action, but the time limit will vary depending on where you live and what someone is alleged to have done. And, of course, it could change, because a law can be amended – unless it's a statue of limitations, in which case it's set in stone.

dull as dishwater

Dishwater *is* pretty dull, isn't it? You stare into it, wondering whether you could have got away with putting the frying pan in the dishwasher, or if it really would have ruined the non-stick surface, as they always warn you. One day you must buy two identical frying pans on the same day and initiate a year-long controlled experiment…

If you think that's dull, try staring into a ditch. It's probably not big enough to contain something as interesting as a shopping trolley, and it hasn't even had an injection of washing-up liquid to hide its dark-souled dankness with light-hearted bubbles.

We can agree that both are dull, but back in the mists of time someone decided that one was duller than the other. So throw out the dishwater and use the right phrase, which is 'dull as ditchwater'.

right of passage

Having 'right of passage' would be a bit like having 'right of way' – in other words, permission to travel via a certain route. However, that isn't what is meant by the correct form of the phrase 'rite of passage'.

Originally, 'rite' referred to a religious ceremony, or a religious observance, but over the centuries it came to denote a custom or practice more generally.

In 1909 the ethnographer Arnold van Gennep published *Les Rites de Passage* (later translated from French into English as *The Rites of Passage*), a work describing rituals which take place when an individual moves from one group of society to another. The phrase entered general usage fairly

soon afterwards, with the most common examples of rites of passage being those related to coming-of-age: religious ceremonies, such as confirmation, bar mitzvah and bat mitzvah; as well as more secular events, such as illegally buying booze, coughing on cigarette smoke and snogging behind the bike sheds (possibly all in the same afternoon).

Trivial Pursuits

Invented by Canadian journalists Chris Haney and Scott Abbott in 1979, though not released until 1981 because it took two years to write the questions, *Trivial Pursuit* is one of the world's most popular board games. So it's weird how many people mistakenly think the title is plural – perhaps because it's not the most logical phrase on its own.

It could have been even less logical, though: they were planning to call it *Trivia Pursuit*, until Haney's wife Sarah suggested adding the 'l'.

You can of course check the correct title using the trivial method of glancing at the box. Once you've done that, you're free to pursue a much more important argument: are you competing for pieces of pie or wedges of cheese?

chomping at the bit

It's 'champing'. Trust me. That is literally what horses do – they grind their teeth together and champ. Champ, champ, champ, champ, champ. That is why the phrase 'to champ at the bit' was invented, to indicate that a horse is impatient and wants to get moving. Possibly because someone has put a load of metal in its mouth and the horse figures that the sooner it gets going, the sooner that same someone will take it out.

Don't start telling me that you Googled it and found millions of hits for 'chomping at the bit' – and, in fact, more hits than for 'champing at the bit' – because then I will tell you that in 1933 millions more people voted for Hitler than any other candidate. Did that make them right?

advanced notice

This is easy to get wrong, because when you notify someone in advance about something, you have brought forward the point in time when they know about it – so you have advanced something. Nevertheless, the correct form is 'advance notice', without the 'd'.

For those who love grammar, the reasoning is that you should be using an adjective ('advance', meaning 'ahead of time') rather than the past participle of the verb 'to advance'. For those who hate grammar, one way to think of this is that you aren't *advancing* the notice itself – you are giving the notice, and the type of notice you are giving is one which is in advance.

Coming back to those who love grammar, they will point out that 'advanced' can also be an adjective. But as an adjective, 'advanced' means 'highly developed' or 'at a higher level' – as in 'an advanced system for taking things a step too far'. In which case, an 'advanced notice' might be some kind of augmented-reality 3D holographic sign in the metaverse, warning you that no one in the metaverse is interested in spelling or grammar.

pour over

If you've carefully examined a dictionary in recent days, then you will know that you were 'poring over' it. If you were 'pouring over' the dictionary, then it's possible that you had involved a bit too much wine, and you probably didn't get as far as the letter P in your haste to mop everything up. (If you were sweating profusely over the dictionary, then that would have meant a lot of fluid emanating from your pores, which might explain your confusion.)

If you haven't been near a dictionary in recent days, or ever, then I can clarify that 'pouring' relates to flowing liquids, while 'poring' involves scrutinising maps, plans or books. And I know what you're thinking: books, hey – whatever happened to them?

'Excuse me while I kiss this guy'

A mondegreen, of which this Jimi Hendrix line is a classic example, is a misheard phrase – usually in song lyrics – which takes on a different meaning from the correct version. The term was coined in a 1954 article for *Harper's Magazine* by Sylvia Wright, in which she recalled listening to her mother read aloud 'The Bonnie Earl o' Moray' to her as a child. The Scottish ballad contains the lines 'They have slain the Earl o' Moray / And layd him on the green.' Wright had always assumed that they had 'slain the Earl Amurray and Lady Mondegreen'.

In the case of the Hendrix song 'Purple Haze', not only is 'kiss this guy' audibly indistinguishable from the correct lyric, it's also just as likely that Hendrix would stop to smooch some random bloke as 'kiss the sky', which is what he actually sings.

If you watch the footage of 'Purple Haze' being performed at the iconic 1969 Woodstock Festival, you see Hendrix briefly pointing upwards while singing the line, appearing to confirm that it's definitely 'the sky'. And if you watch his performance at the 1970 Atlanta Pop Festival, you see him glance upwards immediately after singing it. However, if you believe Harry Shapiro and Caesar Glebbeek, authors of *Jimi Hendrix: Electric Gypsy*, Hendrix was very aware of the confusion and did often sing this live as 'kiss this guy' while pointing at drummer Mitch Mitchell.

marinading

If you're planning to barbecue a load of meat
– or, in my case, a load of tofu – you might
want to *marinate* it in sauce before cooking,
so that it thoroughly absorbs the flavours.
(You might also want to clean the barbecue
while you wait, because you probably didn't
bother to scrape off all the congealed food
last time you finished using it.) The sauce in
question would be a *marinade*.

Like it or not (and I'm absolutely certain you
don't) 'marinate' is a verb, while 'marinade'
is a noun.

By all means go around parading, serenading
or wading – all at the same time, if you want
– but don't go around marinading, as that would
just be degrading. Oh, and don't try to marmelate
your toast, either.

tow the line

This idiom is used to describe someone reluctantly having to follow a specific rule, or to go along with what a particular group decides. Therefore it feels right that it should have its origins in some olde-worlde aspect of towing, like a workhorse pulling a plough, or a burly man using a rope to tow a boat through a canal lock.

However, if you're being forced to go along with something, you wouldn't be towing the line. Someone or something else would be using the line to tow *you*, surely? Which would require you to hold the line, just like Toto back in 1978.

So it's nothing to do with towing; the correct idiom is 'toe the line'. As with many sayings, it's not clear exactly where or when it was first used, but it's very likely to have started in a military context: soldiers or sailors having to line up in a row with their toes neatly aligned with a mark on a parade ground or the edge of a plank.

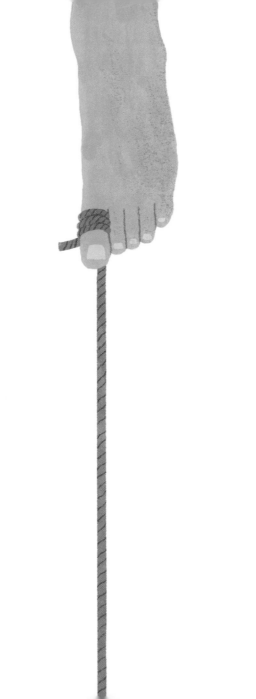

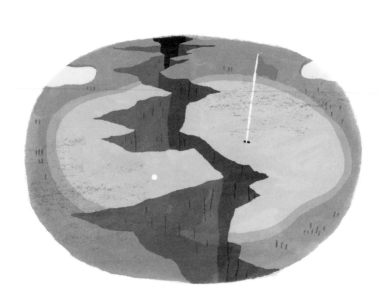

part of the course

Struggling to connect to wifi on a speeding train? Well, that's pretty much what you should expect; it's part of the course.

This sounds logical, in a way: a course of events is unfolding (you are desperately trying to post exciting details of your train journey on social media) and part of that course of events is what you should expect to encounter under typical circumstances (the fact that the train's wifi is so useless that they should just switch it off to set passengers' expectations correctly).

The proper form of this idiom, though, comes from the world of golf. The number of strokes a zero-handicap player needs to complete a hole, or an entire course, is known as the 'par'. If you complete it with more strokes, you're over par, and with fewer strokes, you're under par. But if you complete it with the exact same number of strokes, then you could say you've performed in typical fashion – 'par for the course'.

I could care less

During the twentieth century, this expression emerged as a lazy variant of the original, 'I *couldn't* care less'. This is inexplicable, as 'could' means the opposite of 'couldn't', yet it is used to mean the same thing.

If there is *no possible way in which I could care less* about the celebrity circus of the Kardashians and the Jenners, then I have absolutely no interest in their attention-seeking antics whatsoever.

If there is some way in which I *could* care less about the Kardashian–Jenner dynasty – even if just a tiny, minuscule bit less – then they're not quite at the absolute rock-bottom of my list of celebrities I don't care about. That would leave an opening for me to say that I don't find them quite as tiresome as Prince Harry's attempts to protect his family's privacy by publishing an autobiography and promoting a Netflix series about his family's private life.

To recap: if you really, totally don't like something then you *couldn't* care less about it; but if you *could* care less about it, then you're more interested in it than you thought, and have probably read Prince Harry's autobiography.

nip it in the butt

If you nip something in the bud then you're stopping something from developing – a flower, a shoot, something which grows much bigger – so by acting quickly now, you can prevent a bad habit becoming ingrained and creating a much worse situation later.

By contrast, if you go around nipping butts, you're probably going to be *starting* something, and creating a much worse situation for yourself right now.

all that glitters is not gold

Whether this saying is right or wrong arguably depends on whether you are using it in a modern-day sense or quoting Shakespeare. The Bard of Avon wasn't the first to invoke the idea that shiny stuff isn't necessarily gold and therefore, by extension, that not everything that looks appealing turns out to be as good as it seems; but he devised the aphorism in its best-known form – almost.

The line is spoken by the Prince of Morocco in *The Merchant of Venice*. Embroiled in an elaborate *Deal or No Deal* sub-plot, the prince opens a box containing a scroll, from which he reads: 'All that glisters is not gold.' (Spoiler alert: he doesn't win the top prize.)

Because Shakespeare used the archaic form 'glisters', you're getting this wrong if you're saying 'glitters' while smugly thinking, 'Hey, look at me, quoting the Prince of Morocco!'

If, on the other hand, you're intending to quote a different prince – the purple one who released the single 'Gold' in 1995 – then all that glitters *ain't* gold.

card shark

'Card shark', denoting someone who's extremely good at winning card games (either through skill or by cheating) is a term which has been used so often that it's now pretty much interchangeable with the original form, 'card sharp'. Yes, with a 'p', not a 'k'.

Some of the reason for its spread could be down to the popularity of the American TV game show *Card Sharks*, the title of which was a play on 'card sharps'. (If you're from the UK you might be thinking 'I've never heard of that show.' It was adapted for the Brits as *Play Your Cards Right* – so you *have* actually heard of it, unless you are now trying to claim you don't know who Bruce Forsyth was.)

The *Oxford English Dictionary* first cites 'card sharp' from 1840 ('card shark' was in use by 1877). It also notes that in James Hardy Vaux's *A Vocabulary of the Flash Language*, published in 1819, the word 'sharp' was defined as 'a gambler, or person, professed in all the arts of play; a cheat, or swindler'. Vaux was an incorrigible thief, swindler, forger and deserter who was transported from England to Australia no fewer than three times – so he was definitely a reliable source of information.

pass mustard

Mustard is, obviously, a plant with various uses, best known for the condiment made from its seeds. You could therefore happily pass mustard to someone during a meal if you're at the other end of the table.

However, when you are figuring out whether something is good enough to meet certain criteria, you are, in fact, interested in whether it will pass 'muster'.

This idiom has military origins. A muster is a calling-together of personnel in a particular place for exercise, roll-call or – most relevant in this context – inspection. If an idea passes muster, it successfully bears close scrutiny of all its details.

Unless you're in the military, the nearest you'd get to a muster is probably on a ferry or cruise ship. If you hear the ship's alarm issue seven or more short blasts followed by one long blast, proceed calmly to the muster point, and do not stop to pick up any condiments on the way.

pre-book

'Darling, for your birthday I've just pre-booked
a table at your favourite restaurant,' said
nobody, ever.

That's because the concept of 'pre-booking'
is entirely bogus. It is loved by government
bureaucrats who have bought into Big Tech's
equally bogus concept of 'ride-hailing services'
– a phrase invented so that when the companies
in question attend court cases (something they
seem to enjoy on a daily basis) they can claim
that 'ride-hailing services' are offering something
completely different to what 'taxis' or 'cabs' offer.

Historically, when you wanted to order something
in advance, the details would have been written
down in a book so that later on people could read
who had 'booked' what. Maybe in pre-historic times
they pre-used pre-books for this pre-purpose; but
today if you 'pre-book' something it's the equivalent
of saying you have 'ordered something in advance
in advance'.

extract revenge

Revenge, they say, is a dish best served cold, which would make extracting revenge something like scooping balls of ice cream out of a tub. If that sounds nonsensical, it's because the phrase is not 'extract revenge' at all.

When you want to get revenge, you *exact* it rather than *extract* it. Instead of 'extract', with the sense of taking something out, 'exact' means to demand and obtain something forcefully. As a verb, 'exact' doesn't crop up very often – though you can also exact payment or promises, for example – which is why this gets so confusing.

So now you know. But whether you go for 'exact' or 'extract', I'm sure that eventually you'll get your just desserts.

disinterested

It's pretty unlikely that you need this word often – so if you're using it a lot, you're almost certainly getting it wrong. It isn't about finding something boring.

The 'interested' bit of 'disinterested' relates to the idea of having an interest in something, in the sense that you have some kind of stake in it – usually a financial interest. So if you're disinterested in something, there can be no personal gain to you in what happens to it (if, for example, it is sold) and you could have no bias, or conflict of interest, in making a decision about it.

To better understand this, imagine (it might not be difficult) that you regard the Marvel Cinematic Universe as the most tedious concept anyone has ever come up with. You would therefore be absolutely *un*interested in it. Whereas if you once owned shares in Marvel Studios which you subsequently sold, you would previously have had a financial interest but are now *dis*interested.

For the record, I have never had any interest, in either sense, in the MCU, making me simultaneously disinterested and extremely uninterested.

minefield of information

In its literal sense, a minefield is an area of the ground which is dangerous to walk or drive across because it has been planted with explosive devices. Figuratively, therefore, a minefield is a dangerous situation to be navigated with extreme caution.

However, when people mistakenly talk about a 'minefield of information', what they actually mean is something positive, where information is to be found in abundance. The phrase they've confused it with is, quite simply, 'mine of information', which obviously refers not to explosive devices but to an underground source of something useful or valuable. Think of a gold mine where there are rich pickings to be had, but this mine contains facts and data, rather than a metallic element used to make jewellery which you can send to a PO box for a scammer to melt down without sending you any money in return.

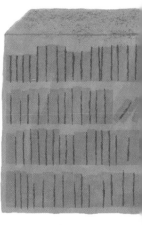

not adverse to

Incompetent train companies like to blame 'adverse weather conditions' when they're inventing excuses about why their trains are so delayed. And corrupt politicians who've been caught claiming expenses for helipad maintenance typically want to avoid 'adverse publicity'.

That's because 'adverse' means 'harmful' or 'having a negative effect' (which, coincidentally, also describes most train companies and politicians).

The 'd' makes all the difference here, because if you are 'averse' to something then you don't like it. So actually, instead of tongue-twistingly saying you're 'not averse to' something, you could simply say you 'like' it – that would save everyone a lot of time and we could all agree to just bin the word 'averse'.

advocado

The name of this fruit – which, botanically speaking, is technically a berry – sounds a bit like it might come from the Spanish word for a lawyer, and in English is often written and pronounced incorrectly as 'advocado', like the start of 'advocate', instead of the correct 'avocado'.

Unsurprisingly, as avocados were first cultivated in what today we might call Latin America, there *is* a Spanish connection, but it's nothing to do with lawyers. The word entered the English language from the Spanish *aguacate*, and earlier English variations included 'avogato', 'avigato', 'avocato' and 'abbogada', as well as the even more garbled concept of the 'alligator pear'. But the Spanish itself derives from the Nahuatl word *ahuacatl*, which is what the Aztecs called it. (Similarly, combining *ahuacatl* with the word *molli*, meaning 'sauce', gave us the word 'guacamole'.)

Some people, far less trustworthy than me, will try to tell you that *ahuacatl* originally meant 'testicle', with the word being used because of a similarity in shape. But that's not true; avocados are definitely fruits and not nuts.

free reign

If someone allows you to do as you please, they're giving you free *rein* – not free *reign*.

The correct spelling, without the 'g', comes from horse-riding: by holding the reins loosely, a rider gives a horse freedom to move as it wishes.

'Reign' refers to ruling, as in a monarch reigning over a country. I suppose you could say you are free to reign over your own opinions, or to overrule other people if they disagree with you, but you'd still be wrong.

Oh, and if you're looking for free *rain*, simply visit Ireland at any time of the year.

irregardless

This is sort of what linguists call a portmanteau word: a single word combined from two or more other words, like 'brunch' or 'labradoodle'. Literally speaking, a portmanteau is a type of bag. We have Humpty Dumpty to thank for its use in this context: in Lewis Carroll's *Through the Looking-Glass*, while explaining the nonsense poem 'Jabberwocky' to Alice, Humpty Dumpty says that 'slithy' ('lithe' and 'slimy') is like a portmanteau because 'there are two meanings packed up into one word'.

The problem here, which makes it only a *sort-of* portmanteau, is that when you merge 'irrespective' and 'regardless' you don't end up with a word which is greater than the sum of its parts in the same way as 'mimsy' ('miserable' and 'flimsy') or 'chortle' ('chuckle' and 'snort'). 'Irregardless' simply isn't a meaningful word; the word you need is 'regardless' because that's what you mean.

Irrespective of whether you agree with me or not, I also need to ask everyone to stop saying 'with regards to' when you mean 'about' (as opposed to sending your best regards). The 's' is wrong. You just need to say 'with regard to'. It's quicker to type, too.

———

pull your socks together

This malapropism is a mix-up between two different idioms which are actually pretty similar. That's why we can easily understand the meaning, even though the image of someone literally pulling their socks together doesn't make a whole lot of sense.

By 'pulling your socks up' you are metaphorically preparing to get something done – with an implication that by letting your socks fall down to begin with, you had taken your eye off the ball. Or the running track. Or something to do with sports, anyway.

'Pulling yourself together' evokes an image of being a bit all over the place, perhaps due to a recent piece of bad news or misfortune, and then regaining your composure.

If in doubt, stick with 'pull yourself together', just so that you can re-tell the timeless joke about the pair of curtains who went to the doctor asking for advice because they were really upset.

baited breath

If you 'bait' something – perhaps a bear or a
badger – you are using dogs to attack it; and,
whilst I hesitate to generalise, I would venture
that you are unlikely to be the kind of person
to be reading a book about words. So I probably
shouldn't be addressing you as 'you' because
you're not reading this. But I'll continue anyway.

'Bate', similar to the verb 'abate' from which it
derives, means to diminish or lower. When you
are anticipating something with a sense of fear
or excitement, you might figuratively be breathing
quietly so as not to disturb whatever it is you think
is round the corner. So, whether it's a scary monster
with two heads or a sequel to a book about words,
you would be waiting for it with bated breath.

pacifically

If you told me *pacifically* not to do something, you'd have instructed me in a peaceful or calm manner. That's because the adverb 'pacifically' comes from 'pacific' – as in the Pacific Ocean, named by the explorer Ferdinand Magellan because of the calm waters he encountered when he first reached it.

If you wanted me not to do something in particular, you should have told me *specifically* not to do it.

There doesn't seem to be any specific, or indeed pacific, reason why some people get this wrong, when one word starts with an 's' sound and the other doesn't. After all, it's not as if people go around saying 'peek' instead of 'speak', or 'pork' instead of 'spork'. Or sperhaps they do and I've just never noticed.

the proof is
in the pudding

Idea for a detective series: in each episode of *Murder, She Ate* a guest star is killed off, with bungling police officers unable to crack the case – until a retired pastry chef uses her culinary skills to catch the perpetrator. There could even be a Magnum crossover episode in which she identifies the murderer via a discarded ice cream stick.

Sadly, this modern-day concept of 'proof' isn't really what this proverb is about, not least because it's not the right proverb. It should be 'the proof of the pudding is in the eating', which gives more of a clue as to its meaning. Historically, 'proof' meant 'testing', not 'definitive evidence'. You can only truly know the quality of a pudding by tasting it – you can't just look at it. In other words, you can only know what something is like by actually experiencing it.

I will reluctantly agree that it doesn't change the meaning much to abbreviate this to 'the proof is in the pudding', even though it's a bit bogus; but only if you will reluctantly agree to finance the first season of *Murder, She Ate*, which is also a bit bogus.

'She drinks a Moët & Chandon'

No, this is *not* the opening line to Queen's 1974 hit 'Killer Queen'. So why do you still sing it, anyway?

The curious thing is that deep down, you've actually known all along that you didn't know the lyric – you just didn't know you knew you didn't know it. That's because you always sing along with the next bit, too. (Don't pretend you don't, because you do.) Why would she drink a Moët & Chandon 'in a pretty cabinet'? Even down in Geisha Minor people don't climb inside cabinets to drink champagne, which is why she *keeps* her Moët & Chandon there.

Then again, incidentally, even Freddie fell foul of the facts when quoting Marie Antoinette in the following line. 'Let them eat cake' is, it turns out, a mistranslation of a phrase about brioche bread. Not so fastidious and precise, after all.

for all intensive purposes

It's far from clear how 'intensive purposes', whatever they might be, relate to the meaning of this phrase, which is, basically, 'basically'.

The correct saying is actually 'to all intents and purposes' – which you might think is no clearer. If it sounds a bit archaic, that's because it is. According to the *Oxford English Dictionary* the phrase first appeared, in a slightly different form, in legislation from the time of England's King Henry VIII. The 1545 Bill Against Usury starts by declaring that all the previous laws which have anything to do with usury

'shall from henceforth be utterly void and of none Effect, to all Intents, Constructions and Purposes.' Over the centuries the 'constructions' fell away (shoddy builders, if you ask me) and speakers also now vary between the original 'to' and 'for'.

So if you've been getting this wrong, you can take heart from the fact that, to all intents and purposes, it's a completely pointless phrase.

Artic/Antartic

Planning a trip to the Artic? If so, you're about to jump into the cab of your articulated lorry.

If what you meant was a visit to the frozen north, then – unless you're an ice road trucker – you want the Arctic, with an extra 'c'.

The name 'Arctic' derives from the Greek word *arktos*, meaning 'bear' – not because there are so many polar bears up there, but because of the northern skies' Great Bear (a constellation variously also known as the Big Dipper, Ursa Major and the Plough).

On the other side of the world, the name 'Antarctic' comes from combining 'anti' (to denote 'opposite') with 'Arctic'. Yes, the 'i' of 'anti' went missing in the process but that still doesn't mean you can drop the 'c'. While 'the Artic' will probably make it through your spellchecker due to the abbreviation for 'articulated', when it comes to 'the Antartic', you're typing on thin ice.

mischevious

I think all of us would spell this word incorrectly more often than we do if we didn't live in a world of autocorrect and predictive text. What a relief to just be able to write 'mischi' and have your phone fill out the rest, while your brain concentrates on the really important stuff, like emojis.

For the record, the modern-day standard spelling is 'mischievous' – and if that has just triggered a flashback from school spelling tests, you're not the only one. It might reassure you to know that the *Oxford English Dictionary* has recorded over twenty different spellings from as far back as the 1500s, including 'mischevieous', 'mischevious', 'mischeivious', 'mischieveous' and 'mischievieous' (no, really – look again, those are all different).

I'm very sympathetic towards everyone who struggles to spell this. One thing I am certain about, however, is its pronunciation. If you think it rhymes with 'previous' and 'devious', you are mistaken. In fact, 'mischievous' doesn't really rhyme with anything.

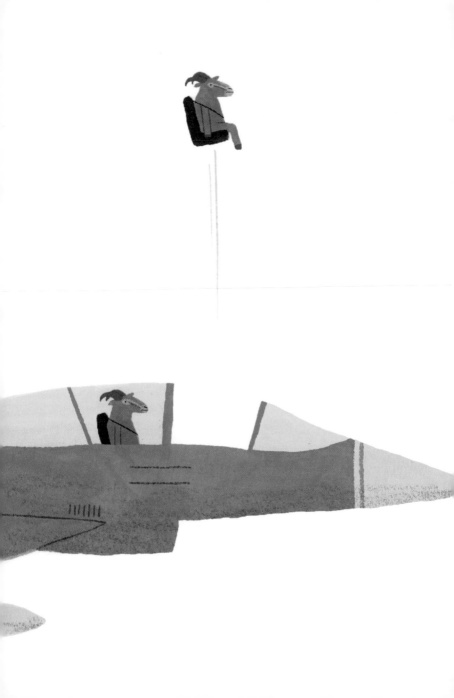

escape goat

The concept of a scapegoat – someone singled out unreasonably for blame – is generally accepted as originating in the Bible, where one of two goats is picked to carry the community's sins before being sent out into the wilderness. (Think the scapegoat got a bad deal? The other goat was sacrificed.)

The term came into being in 1530 as a loose English translation by William Tyndale of the Hebrew word 'azazel'. Scholars disagree as to whether he overlooked the fact that 'azazel' was a reference to a non-Hebrew god, or whether 'azazel' correctly referred to the concept of 'removal'.

One thing *is* certain: in the years before dictionaries, everyone's spelling was all over the place. Tyndale's English looks garbled today: he states that the goat shall 'goo fre in to the wildernesse'. The word we're looking for, which uses the old-school medial 's' (which looks a bit like an 'f') is 'fcapegoote'. And in fact it turns out that Tyndale was really referring to a goat (possibly a gooey one) being allowed to escape. He just wasn't sure about his spelling. Today, though, 'scapegoat' is the form which you'll find in dictionaries.

pronounciation

Whenever I hear this I can't quite tell if the person who says it is doing it deliberately or not. It seems too coincidental that you could really mispronounce a word that describes how you pronounce a word.

You 'pronounce' something, rhyming with the word 'trounce'; and you use 'pronouns' in day-to-day conversation; so 'pronounciation' may seem reasonable. But this noun is written 'pronunciation' and is pronounced (not pronunced) like a convent – with a 'nun' in it.

This explanation was brought to you by the letters 'n', 'o', 'p' and 'u' – and some other less important letters.

damp squid

When something you were expecting to be sensational turns out to be underwhelming, you might say that it fizzled out – which is what a damp squib would do, because a squib is a type of small explosive. If you haven't kept your powder dry, the squib won't explode properly when ignited, leading to a disappointing anti-climax.

On the one hand, I can understand why people might mistakenly think the phrase is 'damp squid' because most of us don't encounter squibs in our day-to-day lives, unless we run a fireworks emporium or work in the film industry (where squibs are often used in special effects such as simulated bullet hits). If the word 'squib' is unfamiliar, it's easy to mishear it as 'squid'.

On the other hand, squids live in water, so if you are actually choosing to describe something as 'like a damp squid', it means it is entirely normal and not disappointing, rendering the phrase completely useless – unless you find yourself continually disappointed by life turning out as expected, in which case I assume you don't care about squids, as you probably have bigger molluscs to fry.

'Play it again, Sam'

This quote, or rather misquote, instantly conjures up the world of the classic 1942 film *Casablanca*: Ingrid Bergman's character asking Dooley Wilson's character, at the piano, to play 'As Time Goes By'. While it accurately summarises what Ilsa is asking of Sam, the line itself isn't actually spoken. Ilsa first says: 'Play it once, Sam. For old times' sake.' After he claims not to know it, she insists: 'Play it, Sam.'

There is no identifiable moment in time at which the different line entered the public consciousness, or a specific person to whom it can be attributed. One thing we do know is that by 1969 it had become sufficiently well known to be used as the title of the Broadway play by Woody Allen, inspired by *Casablanca*, and adapted for film three years later.

A lesser-known fact about *Casablanca* is that it was itself an adaptation of a play. *Everybody Comes to Rick's*, which sounds like the title of an AI-generated sitcom, was written in 1940 by Murray Burnett and Joan Alison, who sold the script to Warner Bros. after they couldn't find a producer willing to stage it. And no, the line 'Play it again, Sam' doesn't feature in the play, either.

———

self-depreciating

The word 'deprecating', which only has one 'i' (think of it as a kind of linguistic cyclops) means 'belittling' or 'disparaging'. By contrast, 'depreciating' (think of it as a kind of linguistic pair of sewing needles) means 'decreasing in value' – like the laptop you only bought two years ago but is apparently now worthless and doesn't support Windows 11, the value of which also seems questionable.

If you're described as 'self-deprecating', it means that you're putting yourself down – usually with the implication that you are underplaying your strengths or achievements for the sake of modesty, often with a bit of humour.

If you're described as 'self-depreciating', however, you should urgently seek advice from a qualified accountant.

unchartered waters

A charter is a document or statement formally recognising and defining the rights or ownership of an organisation or social group. Famous examples include the Charter of the United Nations (the core document defining the purposes and structure of the UN), first ratified in 1945, and England's *Magna Carta* (which is Medieval Latin for 'great charter'), agreed with King John in 1215.

You might therefore think if you venture into 'unchartered territory' or 'unchartered waters' that these are unfamiliar because they haven't been legally granted to anyone by charter – no one knows anything about them yet.

Actually, though, you're just using too many letters, because you should be venturing into 'uncharted territory' and 'uncharted waters'. The correct expression comes from the noun 'chart', in its older sense of a map or a plan, and hence the verb 'to chart', meaning to record on a map or a plan. So if you're in uncharted waters, you're travelling somewhere which hasn't yet been mapped.
And by the way, I hope you've paid for the boat hire – otherwise you might be sailing an unchartered vessel.

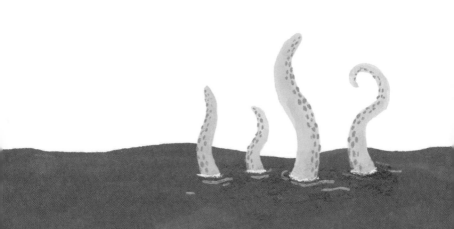

alot

This expression is actually two words: 'a lot'. It's as simple as that! In this context, 'lot' means 'large amount'. You wouldn't write about 'alargeamount'. Or maybeyouwould.

Why do so many people write this as a single word? Can it be confusion with the fact that 'allot' is a real word? That has an extra 'l' and means something completely different – to give out a portion of something – so it seems unlikely.

There is, of course, the copycat factor: if you've seen a lot (or alot) of other people write it as one word, you might end up doing the same. It could also be that people think of it as a single word because 'lot' on its own isn't really used in the sense of 'large amount' without the preceding 'a'. You might write about your favourite parking lot or that expensive lot you nearly bought at auction, but it's usually a lot of hot air. So, remember that it's two words, the lot of you.

slight of hand

As with 'right' versus 'rite', it's easy to see why the incorrect spelling of 'slight' is often confused with the correct spelling of 'sleight', because they are homophones: they are pronounced the same way but mean different things. (They derive from quite distinct Old Norse words but have ended up nearly identical in English.) It's even more understandable when there isn't really any modern-day use for the word 'sleight' other than in the phrase 'sleight of hand'.

'Slight', as an adjective, means small; and as a noun it can denote a display of indifference or contempt. But when it comes to the art of conjuring – better known as 'out-of-work actors irritating people with magic tricks' – sleight of hand is essential, to skilfully ensure the performer's technique goes undetected.

expresso

As you are doubtless aware, this method of making coffee originated in Italy. What might be less obvious is that the Italian alphabet doesn't utilise the letter 'x', except for words taken from other languages, so this type of coffee is named *caffè espresso* in Italian, abbreviated to simply *espresso*.

The English translation of *espresso* is 'expressed'. Both the Italian word and its English equivalent have multiple connotations: in this context the meaning is 'pressed out' (the flavour of the coffee

emerges under steam pressure); but there is also perhaps an implication of 'speed' (the coffee is prepared quickly).

Of course, when it comes to coffee, everyone loves to bandy about Italian words like *macchiato*, *latte* and *ristretto*, so we also just use the word *espresso* in English – with an 's', not an 'x'. Which makes sense, because even if you tried to use an English translation, it would be 'expressed' and not 'expresso'. So please stop saying 'expresso'. If you can't manage that, then just order a 'cup of chino' instead.

revert

There's nothing wrong with the word 'revert' – normally. It can mean 'to turn back into', as in: 'He reverted to his usual nit-picking self.' Referring to a legal sense of ownership, it can mean 'to pass back to', as in: 'Due to a lack of interest by the publisher, the rights reverted to the author.'

However, in recent years a new meaning has crept into corporate communication which is extremely irritating: people using 'I will revert to you', or simply 'I will revert', to mean that they will respond to you later once they have more information. Just like 'I'll get back to you', a phrase which already exists and which there was no need to replace.

If you say you will revert to me, you're basically saying that at some future point you will be turning back into me. That makes no sense, because not only can you not become me, but you never were me to begin with – something for which I'm very grateful because that would presumably mean that I was you. And I don't want to be you because you use the word 'revert' incorrectly.

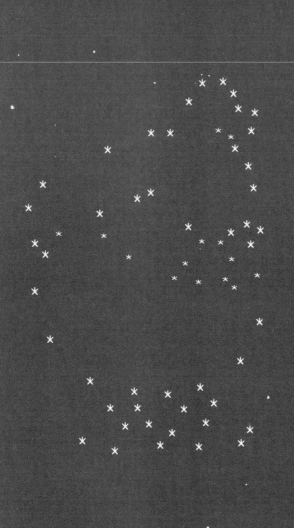

asterix

It's amazing how often people confuse the star symbol* with the moustachioed comic book character from Gaul. This is undoubtedly down to a pronunciation mix-up between the sounds 'ix' and 'isk' – a phenomenon, or phemonemom, known to linguists as metathesis.

The asterisk has a variety of typographical uses, from enabling advertisers to legally point out in small print that the claim they've just made is in fact completely untrue, to allowing writers to get away with swearing like f***ing troopers.

In 2022 tennis legend Martina Navratilova dipped her toe in the waters of cancel culture by suggesting that trans athletes should be distinguished by the use of an asterisk after their names. If this proposal is adopted, I'll be keenly awaiting the revised edition of *Asterisk at the Olympic Games*.

*The English word 'asterisk' ultimately derives from the Ancient Greek for 'little star'.

wet my appetite

The idea here is that my appetite is stimulated; perhaps I've just scoffed a canapé at a dreary networking event and only now do I realise I would rather be somewhere else, eating a massive burger with onion rings, loaded fries and dill pickles on the side. (Incidentally, by 'canapé' I am thinking of a tiny slice of basil on top of a tiny slice of tomato on top of a tiny slice of mozzarella on top of a tiny slice of circular toast – not a tiny sofa.)

My enthusiasm for something is, figuratively, sharpened by an initial taste. It's sharpening that's meant by the correct spelling of the verb 'whet', with an 'h'. Literally, you can whet a knife or the blade of a tool, which is what a whetstone is used for.

Perhaps I could try to wet my appetite by drinking some wine before I go for my massive burger – awkwardly holding a tiny napkin, wine glass and my business card in one hand, while I scoff my canapé with the other hand and try to 'network' with someone by mumbling my name through a mouthful of toast, mozzarella, tomato and basil. But wetting my enthusiasm would dampen it, which is the opposite of what 'whet my appetite' means.

———

tender hooks

If you're in a state of nervous tension, you might say that you're 'on tender hooks'. You're probably wondering what a tender hook is. I certainly am.

A hook needs to have some kind of rigidity, as it's for hanging and attaching things – so a soft and floppy hook wouldn't stand up to much scrutiny. (Stop smirking.) And this saying doesn't have anything to do with other meanings of the word 'tender', such as money ('legal tender') or steam trains (where a 'tender' would contain water and coal), because you should actually be on 'tenterhooks'.

Now you're wondering what a tenterhook is. I won't leave you hanging: it's a type of nail used on a tenter.

All right, all right... now you want to know what a 'tenter' is! I just wanted to build up the suspense.

A tenter is a frame which, historically, was used in the production of cloth. After being washed, the cloth would be stretched out on the tenter, using tenterhooks, to prevent it deforming as it dried. That's why being 'on tenterhooks' came to mean being 'stretched', 'uneasy' or 'nervous'.

And relax.

acknowledgements

Many thanks to all those who helped, directly or indirectly, in the creation of this book: Sarah Lavelle, for bringing it into the world; Daniel Rieley, for his excellent visual flair; Alicia House, for the wonderful design work; Sofie Shearman, for keeping things moving efficiently; Wendy Hobson, for her valuable edit; Anna Watson, for her proofreader's eye; Kate Pool and the Society of Authors for 'business stuff'; and various family and friends for their support and ideas (even if I didn't manage to remember them…), including Karen Jeger, James 'advanced' Sleigh, Niall and Jody Jeger, Dave Meaden, Patrick 'pre-book' Rodger and Alex 'part of the course' Bridge.

about the author

Robert Anwood is a writer and musician based in London. He is the author of *Bears Can't Run Downhill* and *Emus Can't Walk Backwards*, and is the keyboard player for indie band Jody and the Jerms, with whom he has recorded the albums *Deeper*, *Flicker* and *Wonder*.

managing director
Sarah Lavelle

assistant editor
Sofie Shearman

designer
Alicia House

illustrator
Daniel Rieley

head of production
Stephen Lang

senior production controller
Katie Jarvis

Published in 2023 by Quadrille, an imprint of Hardie Grant

Quadrille
52–54 Southwark Street
London SE1 1UN
quadrille.com

Cataloguing in Publication Data: a catalogue record for
this book is available from the British Library.

ISBN 978 1 83783 085 5
Printed in China